Books in the Linkers series

Homes discovered through Art & Technology
Homes discovered through Geography
Homes discovered through History
Homes discovered through Science

Myself discovered through Art & Technology
Myself discovered through Geography
Myself discovered through History
Myself discovered through Science

Toys discovered through Art & Technology
Toys discovered through Geography
Toys discovered through History
Toys discovered through Science

Water discovered through Art & Technology
Water discovered through Geography
Water discovered through History
Water discovered through Science

First paperback edition 1996
First published 1996 in hardback by A&C Black (Publishers) Limited
35 Bedford Row, London WC1R 4JH

ISBN 0-7136-4581-4
A CIP catalogue record for this book is available from the British Library.

Commissioned photographs by Zul Mukhida
Design by Jean Wheeler
Picture research by Liz Harman

Acknowledgements

Lesley and Roy Adkins; 3 (right), 5 (right), Adrian Arbib; 2, Advertising Archives; 8/9, 15 (right), 17 (left), 20 (right), 21, Beamish; 8 (left) and cover, 10, 12 (right), 13, 14, 17 (right), 18, 20 (left), Eye Ubiquitous; 5 (left), 7, Hulton Deutsch; 15 (left), Robert Opie; 11 (left), 16, Positive Images; 6 (left), 19 (right), 23 (left), Tony Stone; Ed Pritchard 22, Topham; 9 (right), Triton; 19 (left), Zefa; 3 (left), 6 (right), 23 (right).

Printed and bound in Italy by L.E.G.O.

Homes

discovered through

History

Karen Bryant-Mole

Contents

A & C Black • London

Homes through time

People have always needed somewhere to live.
Where you live is called your home.

Caves
Caves were some of the earliest homes.
Thousands of years ago, people lived in these caves.
They made pictures of animals on the rocks outside.

Huts

This hut has been built to look like the type of home that people might have lived in about nine hundred years ago. The walls are made from wood. The roof is made from reeds.

Today

Today's homes often have lots of rooms.
Many homes are made of bricks.
They usually have glass windows.

This book will take a closer look at the way our homes and the things in them have changed over the last one hundred years.

3

Designs

Over the years, building styles and fashions have changed. You can often guess how old a home is just by looking at it.

One hundred years old
This house was built about a hundred years ago.
It has sash windows that slide up and down.
Its bricks are covered with smooth plaster, called stucco.

Sixty years old

The house below is about sixty years old.
Its bricks are covered with pebbledash, which is a mixture of stones and concrete.
It has a front garden and a back garden.

Thirty years old

This block of flats is about thirty years old.
It is made from big blocks of concrete.
It is very tall and has a boxy look to it.

Why not find out when your home was built?

Materials

Some of the materials used to build homes, such as bricks and glass, have stayed much the same over the last one hundred years. Others have changed.

Wood
This 1900s home has wooden window frames. Wooden frames have to be looked after and painted or they will rot.

Metal
Here are some homes that were built in the 1950s.
They have metal window frames.
Metal frames became unpopular because they sometimes went rusty.

Plastic

The people who live in this home are replacing their windows frames with frames made from a special type of plastic.

Many of the new homes that are built today have plastic window frames like this. Plastic frames are easy to look after and do not have to be painted.

Indoors

Over the years, the ways in which we choose to decorate our homes have changed.

Rich colours

A hundred years ago, it was fashionable to decorate your home in deep, rich colours and hang many pictures on the walls.
People had lots and lots of ornaments, too.
Today, this room would seem rather overcrowded.

Pale colours

By the 1930s it was fashionable to decorate your rooms in pale colours. People liked soft pinks, blues, yellows and greens. Rooms looked bright and airy.

Patterns

In the 1960s, many people liked big, bold patterns. They often had patterned wallpaper, carpets and curtains. Bright oranges and purples were popular colours.

How are the rooms in your home decorated?

In the kitchen

People usually do all their cooking in the kitchen.

Range
A hundred years ago, most people used a type of cooker called a range. It was heated by a coal or wood fire.

Food is cooking in a pan above this fire. Behind the round door is an oven.

Storing food

Few people had electricity in their homes.
People stored their food in a cool cupboard,
called a larder.

This jar is made from a type of pottery known
as stoneware.
Food and drinks were often kept in stoneware jars
and pots.

Electricity

This advert for an electric
cooker appeared in
the 1960s.
By then, almost all homes
had electricity.
Electric cookers were
cleaner than ranges and
the heat was easier
to control.

In the wash house

Clothes used to be washed in a room called a scullery or in a wash house. Today, we usually do the washing in the kitchen or utility room.

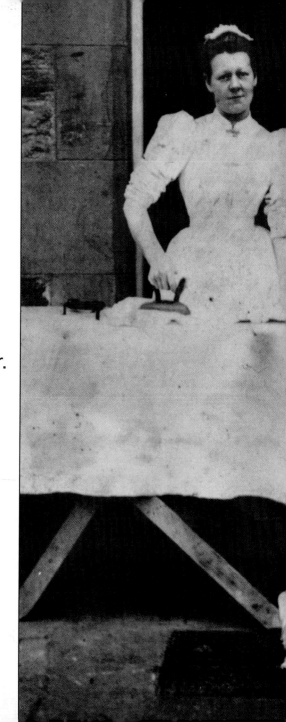

Washing by hand

One hundred years ago, all washing was done by hand.

The clothes were put into a tub of water. A washing dolly, like the one on the left, was used to swish the water through the clothes.

Maids

People who were well-off usually had maids to do the laundry.

One of these girls is using a washing dolly. The other is ironing clothes, using an iron that was heated up on the range.

Washing machines

Many of the early washing machines had to be filled with buckets of water.

This 1950s machine did not spin the clothes. The clothes had to be put between two rollers which squeezed out the water.

In the living room

A hundred years ago, this room would have been called the
Today, we call it a living room, sitting room or lounge.

Parlour
The parlour was
the best room
in the house.
It was always kept
neat and tidy, in case
visitors called.

Children were never
allowed to play in
the parlour.

Family room

By the 1940s, the living room had become a room for all the family.

This family is sitting around a radio.

There were lots of special radio programmes for children.

Very few families had a television set.

Television

Nowadays, most homes have a television in the living room.

This television was made in the 1950s.

It only showed pictures in black and white.

In the dining room

Throughout the years, the dining room has been a special room where meals are eaten.

Crockery
Plates, bowls, cups and saucers are all known as crockery. Different styles of crockery have been popular over the years.

This jazzy style, called Art Deco, was very popular in the 1920s and 1930s.

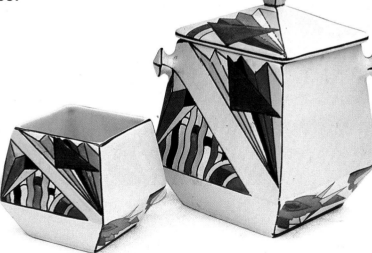

Meals

The picture on the right was taken in 1937.

The mother would have bought or grown everything for the meal and then cooked it herself.

Today we can choose to buy things like ready-made meals and frozen chips.

Entertaining

This woman is laying the table, ready for a dinner party.

Inviting friends to dinner parties was a fashionable thing to do in the 1950s.

Magazines and books showed people how to cook exciting meals.

In the bathroom

A hundred years ago, most homes were built without a bathroom.

Bathtub
Can you see a metal bathtub hanging on the wall of this backyard? A hundred years ago, baths like this were brought inside and filled with buckets of hot water.

On cold days, the bath was placed in front of the coal fire to keep the bather warm.

Toilets

The toilet on the right is in a shed in the garden of a house.

Eighty years ago, most homes only had an outside toilet.

Instead of soft toilet paper, people had to use hard, scratchy paper.

Some people used squares of newspaper!

Today

Today's homes are built with shower rooms, bathrooms and even little bathrooms off bedrooms.

In the bedroom

Today, as in the past,
our bedrooms have beds and
places to store our clothes.
But some things about bedrooms
have changed.

Hot water bottle
This hot water bottle is made
from stoneware.
It is about a hundred years old.
It was filled with hot water and
then put into the bed to warm it.

Blankets
The bed in this 1940s picture
has sheets and blankets.
Over the top, there is a cover,
called a bedspread.
Nowadays, most people have
a duvet on their bed.

Heat

Today's bedrooms are usually warmed by radiators. In the 1950s, most bedrooms had no heating at all. This lady has a soft mat to step on to and cosy slippers to keep her feet warm.

My home

Homes are often
changed over the years.

Extensions
Sometimes the changes
alter the shape
of the home.
An extra room has
been built on to
this home.
This is called
an extension.

Flats

Some changes happen inside the home.
Sometimes a big house is made into several smaller flats.

Decorating

People like their homes to look fashionable.
Fashions change and so people redecorate their homes.

Why not find out how your home has been changed since it was first built?

Think about the way it is decorated and the things that you have in it, as well as any building work that might have been done.

Glossary

bold large, strong
control make something do what you
  want it to
ornaments decorations
overcrowded too many things in too
  small a space

reed the long, thin stem of a plant
  that grows near water
sash windows windows with two main
  parts that are opened by pulling the
  top part down or the bottom part up

Index

How to use this book

Each book in this series takes a familiar topic or theme and focuses on one area of the curriculum: science, art and technology, geography or history. The books are intended as starting points, illustrating some of the many different angles from which a topic can be studied. They should act as springboards for further investigation, activity or information seeking.

The following list of books may prove useful.

Further books to read

Series	Title	Author	Publisher
Changing Times	Cooking Housework	R. Thomson	Watts
Daily Life ...	Daily Life in a Victorian House Daily Life in a Wartime House	L. Wilson	Heinemann
Explainers	Homes and Houses Long Ago	H. Edom	Usborne
History from Objects	In the Home	K. Bryant-Mole	Wayland
History from Photographs	Houses and Homes In the Home	Cox & Hughes	Wayland
History Mysteries	Bathtime; Bedtime Cleaning; Washing	Tanner & Wood	A&C Black
Living in the ...	all titles	Rees & Maguire	Heinemann
People through History	People at Home	K. Bryant-Mole	Wayland

Timeline
You can use this timeline to work out how long ago the things in this book were made and to compare the ages of different items.

nearly 120 years ago	nearly 110 years ago	nearly 100 years ago	nearly 90 years ago	nearly 80 years ago	nearly 70 years ago	nearly 60 years ago	nearly 50 years ago	nearly 40 years ago	nearly 30 years ago	nearly 20 years ago	nearly 10 years ago
the 1880s	the 1890s	the 1900s	the 1910s	the 1920s	the 1930s	the 1940s	the 1950s	the 1960s	the 1970s	the 1980s	the 1990s
1880	1890	1900	1910	1920	1930	1940	1950	1960	1970	1980	1990